HOW IN THE WORLD IS THAT VEGAN & GLUTEN-FREE?!

100% PLANT-BASED COMFORT FOOD RECIPES THAT WILL BLOW YOUR MIND!

EILEEN BATES

HOW IN THE WORLD IS THAT VEGAN AND GLUTEN-FREE?!

Copyright © 2019 Eileen Bates

All rights reserved. No part of this book may be used or reproduced by any means, graphic, electronic, or mechanical, including photocopying, recording, taping or by any information storage retrieval system without the written permission of the author except in the case of brief quotations embodied in critical articles and reviews.

ISBN 978-1-945169-22-9

Front Cover and Interior Design by:
Rachel13 Design
www.Rachel13.com

Cartoon People Illustrated by:
Leah Trevillyan
@scarlettrevster on Instagram

Photography: Eileen Bates
www.batesphoto.net

Orison Publishers, Inc.
PO Box 188
Grantham, PA 17027
717-731-1405
www.OrisonPublishers.com
Publish your book now,
marsha@orisonpublishers.com

INTRODUCTION

When people transition into a plant-based lifestyle, they feel they are giving up quite a bit. Yet after awhile they realize how amazing they feel and there is just no going back! This is exactly how I felt after only two months on a plant-based diet.

The first year of my transition was dedicated to finding foods that were tasty and met all my requirements. I was so desperate and longing for a good hearty meal. When you are gluten-free and vegan it's difficult to find things that are satisfying and filling. My friends would constantly ask "What do you eat all day?" I would always reply, "I'm still trying to figure it all out." Then, into my second year, I felt confident enough to start challenging myself to experiment in the kitchen and find the tastes that I remembered and missed. Somehow I did it! I couldn't believe how foods that would normally be filled with dairy and other animal products could now be made in a vegan and gluten-free version without compromising the taste.

I'm so thrilled to have created a cookbook with hearty vegan and gluten-free recipes inside that are super easy to make. I should tell you that I'm not a chef. I'm just a normal woman who decided to go vegan and gluten-free for health reasons. I had to educate myself about alternative products that were free of dairy, eggs, gluten, and even soy. When I find something good, I like to share it with the world! I list the products I use throughout this book that I feel are best in the recipes. I am not sponsored or affiliated with any of these companies. I do, however, support products that are organic and non-gmo and are minimally processed. Thank you for picking this book up and allowing me to share some of my yummy recipes with you.

Eileen Bates

ACKNOWLEDGMENTS

To my amazing husband and love of my life Dan: Thank you for giving me wings to soar. You are my everything. I love you beyond words! You and me...spanning time.

To my wonderful daughter Alyssa: Thank you for being my taste tester and photo critic. I love our trips to MOM's Organic Market and our mission to use less plastic. I'm so proud of you and love you very much!

To my loving parents (aka Mommy & Daddy): Saying thank you is just not enough to let you know the gratitude I have for all you do for me. I love you so much. You both are my rock!

To my fabulous designer and sister Rachel: You are the best graphic designer in the world! I knew from the start that I wanted you to design this cookbook and wow just wow! I love you and thank you so much!!

To Dave and Maddie: Love you both! Thanks for always listening to me ramble on about all things vegan and gluten-free! Thank you for loving my cupcakes! Tell Meals, Vera, Eli, and Sylvia that Aunt Bean loves them very much!

To my vegan soul sister Dorothea: You have shown love and support to me for as long as I can remember and we have an "arch of light" connecting us always. You mean the world to me and I love you very much. Thank you for joining me from the beginning in this passion for veganism and the animals!

To MY KIMMY: Thank you for being an earth angel of love, laughter, and shear fun! You always have supported my endeavors and you are so dear to me! You are perfection MY KIMMY!!! LOVE YOU!!!

To Erich (aka Fong): We have been on an awesome journey as friends and I know it will continue long into the future! You always challenge me to be my best self! It's a blast being a "foodie" with you and trying out new and exciting flavors. "I know everything there is to know about you and my memory is long".

To the one and only Mandy: Thank you for always taking an interest in my crazy projects! I love having our "night owl" conversations and your support has been awesome! You are the other pea in my pod, a friend, an awesome voice teacher colleague, and an all around DIVA in the best meaning of that word!

To the wonderful Nikki: Thank you for all of your super kind feedback when I show my food photos! You have such a loving personality and care for animals so deeply! I love our spiritual group and our fun times together! Thank you for just being you!

To Leah: It was so awesome having you contribute your artistic and graphic skills to this project! Thank you so much and just know that I was thrilled with your amazing designs of my cartoon self and James Aspey!

To Marsha: Thanks so much for everything you've done! Your time and dedication to this project has been a true blessing! I'm grateful to have Orison as my publisher!

To Sherri: You are the best neighbor, friend, and family member that anyone could ask for. You inspire me! You have dealt with eating Gluten-Free long before people even knew about it. Thanks for being a big part of my life! Love you always!

To my cousins Colleen and Sean: Thank you both so much for your support and encouragement when I first told you I was about to embark on this cookbook project! Love you!

To Mason: Love you buddy! Can't believe how tall you are! Love, Aunt Eileen

To Kira: Love you Girl! Love our Facetime conversations and our special Chincoteague Turtle song! Love, Aunt Eileen

To James Aspey: Thank you for your beautiful quote on the back cover. Your work as an activist inspires so many people to look at the truth in a direct but gentle way. Your words are a gift to mankind and the animals!

CONTENTS

SOUPS SIDES and SNACKS — 9

Cheesy Cheddar Potato and Onion Soup 11
The Best Tomato Soup 12
Sweet Onion, Corn and Potato Soup 15
Creamy Spinach and Onions 17
Buttery Mashed Potatoes 18
Organic Maple Butter Carrots 20
Cheesy Sweet Onion Rice 23
Great Guacamole 24
Air Fried Potato Cakes 27
Cream Cheese Fruit Dip 28
Mozzarella Cheese and Garlic Biscuits 31

ENTREÉS — 33

Spectacular Sausage Spaghetti Sauce 35
Amazing Avocado Burger Club 36
Pineapple Onion Fajitas 38
Creamy Spinach Penne 41
Wonderful Belgium Waffles 42
Avocado Toast 45
Sausage and Garlic Fried Rice 47
Homemade Organic Corn Tortillas with "Beef" 48
Cheesy Garlic Alfredo Pasta 50
5-Ingredient Stovetop Mac N Cheese 52
Sensational Sloppy Joes 54

DESSERTS — 57

Classic Chocolate Chip Cookies 59
Blissful Banana Bread 60
Cinnamon Sugar Corn Tortillas with Chocolate Chip Cream Cheese Dip 62
Chocolate Cupcakes 65
Easy Buttercream Icing 66
Carrot Cake with Cream Cheese Glaze 68
Chocolate Covered Frozen Banana Bites with Sea Salt 70
Fudge Brownies 72
Vanilla and Chocolate Milkshakes 75
Warm Cinnamon Banana Delight 76
Scrumptous Bread Pudding 79

DRINKS — 81

Amazing Blueberry Cheesecake Smoothie 83
Chocolate Covered Banana Smoothie 84
Hot Mulled Apple Cidar 87
Organic Orange and Pineapple Smoothie 88
Peaches N Cream Smoothie 90
Perfect Chocolate Milk 93
Banana Almond Butter Smoothie 94
Refreshing Organic Limeade 97
Organic Blueberry Lemonade 98

CHEESY CHEDDAR, POTATO, and ONION SOUP

This soup is so rich and cheesy and just marvelous! I finally found a really good brand of vegan cheese that actually tastes like CHEESE! Thank you Violife!

WHAT YOU'LL NEED:
1/2 organic sweet onion
4 small organic potatoes
2 organic carrots
2 Tbsp organic olive oil
2 Tbsp vegan butter (I love Miyoko's)
2 cups filtered water
1 cup unsweetened almond milk (I like Malk)
4 slices of Violife Mature Cheddar
A dash of garlic powder
Salt and pepper to taste

*Serves 4

DIRECTIONS:
Prep work: Peel and cube potatoes, chop onion, and cut carrots into small even pieces. In a medium saucepan on medium heat, drizzle the olive oil on the bottom of pan and add onions. Cook until onions are translucent (about 3-5 minutes). Add potatoes, carrots, butter, water, and almond milk. Stir and bring to a boil then reduce heat to a simmer. Add your cheese by tearing each slice into small pieces and place into pot. Cover with lid and let simmer for 15 minutes or until potatoes are soft. Once they are ready, turn heat off and add your seasoning. Note: Be generous with the salt and pepper as it brings out the flavors. Take a stick blender and blend until desired consistency. Let rest a few minutes. Add some roasted onions on top (optional) and serve this deliciousness!

HOW IN THE WORLD IS THAT VEGAN & GLUTEN-FREE?!

The BEST Tomato Soup

The title says it all! This is absolutely the best tomato soup I have ever tried!

WHAT YOU'LL NEED:

24 oz bottle of organic strained tomatoes (I love Bionaturae)
1/4 of a package of vegan butter (I only use Miyoko's)
1 cup unsweetened almond milk (I like Malk)
3/4 tsp sea salt (more or less to taste)
2 Tbsp organic cane sugar (more or less to taste)

* Serving Size 3-4

DIRECTIONS:

In a small saucepan, combine all ingredients over medium heat for approx 3 minutes. Stir thoroughly. Once fully heated, serve and enjoy this amazing soup. It doesn't get any easier than that!

SWEET ONION, CORN and POTATO SOUP

This soup is a dream on a cold day. So rich and flavorful, nobody will believe this is vegan and gluten-free!

WHAT YOU'LL NEED:

3 Tbsp organic olive oil
1/2 package of Miyoko's Cultured Vegan Butter
2 medium sweet onions
3 small organic potatoes (I prefer Yukon gold)
1 package frozen organic super sweet corn (I prefer Woodstock brand)
3 cups filtered water
2 cups unsweetened almond milk (I prefer Malk)
2 Tbsp sea salt (you can adjust amount to your taste)
1 tsp ground pepper
4 Tbsp organic cane sugar (you can sweeten to taste)

*Serves 5

DIRECTIONS:

First, chop up the onions and cube the potatoes. Turn on burner to medium-high heat. In your saucepan, drizzle olive oil to coat bottom of pan and add Miyoko's butter. Once butter is melted, add the onions and potatoes stirring frequently until onions turn translucent (approx 5 minutes). Add the water, almond milk, frozen corn, salt and pepper. Bring to a boil and reduce to medium-low heat. Cover and let simmer for 15 minutes. Turn off heat and with a stick blender puree soup to desired consistency. Add sugar to taste. Serve and enjoy!

Creamy SPINACH and ONIONS

What a perfect side dish to complement any dinner. Great for Thanksgiving!

WHAT YOU'LL NEED:
2 Tbsp organic olive oil
1/2 of a sweet organic onion
1/4 cup vegan butter (I love Miyoko's)
1 tsp organic minced garlic (I use the Christopher Ranch brand)
1/3 cup vegan cream cheese (I use Violife for this dish)
1 cup unsweetened almond milk (I love Malk)
1 large organic baby spinach package (I use Olivia's 11oz)

*Serves 4

DIRECTIONS:
Chop your onion and turn on your burner to a medium high heat. In a medium to large saucepan, coat the bottom of the pan with olive oil. Next, place the onions in the pan and cook until translucent (about 3 minutes). Add the butter, garlic, and cream cheese and lower the heat. Stir together until all is melted. Add the almond milk and begin to add your baby spinach a little at a time and continue until you use the entire container. Stir for a few minutes until all spinach is wilted. Serve and enjoy!

HOW IN THE WORLD IS THAT VEGAN & GLUTEN-FREE?!

BUTTERY Mashed Potatoes

WHAT YOU'LL NEED:
6 medium organic potatoes (I like organic Yukon gold)
1/2 cup vegan butter (I always use Miyoko's)
1/4 cup unsweetened almond milk (I like Malk)
Garlic powder, salt, and pepper to taste

*Serves 4

DIRECTIONS:
Peel and cube your potatoes and place in saucepan. Cover with cold water until all potatoes are submerged. Bring water to a boil and cook for 20 minutes or until potatoes are soft. Strain potatoes and return to saucepan. Add the butter and unsweetened almond milk and mash together. Add the garlic powder, salt, and pepper to taste. Serve and enjoy!

These mashed potatoes are so delicious and a staple in my house. Bring these to any holiday dinner and your friends and family will be shocked to learn they are vegan!

HOW IN THE WORLD IS THAT VEGAN & GLUTEN-FREE?!

ORGANIC MAPLE BUTTER CARROTS

You will find that these carrots are simply magnificent tasting! A perfect side dish for any meal. Very easy to make and makes a statement when you serve these carrots whole!

WHAT YOU'LL NEED:
1 bunch of organic carrots (preferably thin and a longer length)
3 Tbsp organic maple syrup
1 Tbsp vegan butter (I love and highly recommend Miyoko's)
1/3 cup filtered water
Salt and Pepper to taste

* Serving Size 3

DIRECTIONS:
Cut the leafy top part of the carrots off (save a few for a garnish) leaving about 1/2 inch at the top. Clean your carrots with a vegetable brush and remove any strings or excess at the carrot points. Place cleaned carrots into a non-stick pan. Add butter and stir over medium heat for about 1 minute. Add water and maple syrup and bring to a quick boil then reduce heat to medium-low and cover with lid. Set timer for 15-20 minutes or until carrots are slightly soft. That's literally all there is to it!! Serve and enjoy these amazing carrots!

Cheesy SWEET ONION RICE

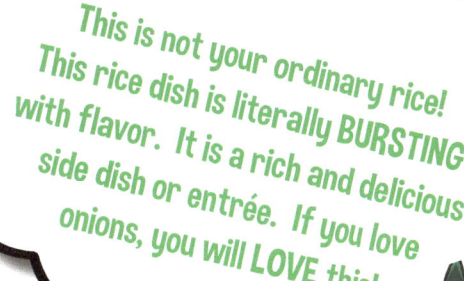

This is not your ordinary rice! This rice dish is literally BURSTING with flavor. It is a rich and delicious side dish or entrée. If you love onions, you will LOVE this!

WHAT YOU'LL NEED:
1 medium sweet organic onion
2 Tbsp organic olive oil
3 Tbsp vegan cream cheese (I enjoy Violife)
1/4 cup vegan butter (I love Miyoko's)
1 cup filtered water
1/2 cup unsweetened almond milk (I love Malk)
1/4 tsp garlic powder
Salt and pepper to taste
1 cup organic long grain rice

*Serves 4

DIRECTIONS:
Chop your onion and put a medium size saucepan on your burner. Over high heat, drizzle the olive oil into the saucepan. Place the onions into the pan and stir well. Cook the onions for about 3-5 minutes or until they are translucent. Reduce heat to medium low and add the cream cheese and butter until it melts together. Once melted, add the water and almond milk and stir for about 5 minutes. Add the garlic powder, salt and pepper to your taste. Once you have achieved the perfect seasoned taste, add the rice to this sauce (rinse rice first). Bring heat back to high for a few minutes until everything comes to a boil. Place a tight fitting lid on pot and reduce heat to a simmer. Set your timer for 15 minutes. Once the timer rings, take rice off heat and let it rest with lid still on for approx 15 minutes. Lastly, fluff rice with fork and serve!

HOW IN THE WORLD IS THAT VEGAN & GLUTEN-FREE?!

GREAT GUACAMOLE

Not all guacamoles are the same. This recipe happens to be one GREAT Guac!

WHAT YOU'LL NEED:
3 organic avocados
1 organic lime
1/2 of a small organic onion
4 Tbsp organic cilantro
1 small organic tomato
1/2 tsp salt
Garlic powder and pepper to taste

* Serving Size 2-3

DIRECTIONS:
Cut your avocados in half and scoop out onto a plate. With a fork, mash your avocados well. Add salt, pepper, and garlic powder to the mashed avocado to your taste and set aside. Finely chop the onion, cilantro, and tomato. In a small mixing bowl, juice your lime. Next, place mashed avocado and the rest of ingredients into bowl and stir well. Finally, add more seasoning to mixture if needed and serve. Enjoy the deliciousness with some corn tortillas as pictured.

AIR FRIED POTATO CAKES

(an air fryer is needed for this recipe)

This is the perfect way to use up those leftover vegan mashed potatoes! Yummy!

WHAT YOU'LL NEED:
2 cups leftover vegan mashed potatoes
(mashed potatoes should have been refrigerated)
2 Tbsp vegan cream cheese (I like Miyoko's Plainly Classic)
1 Tbsp unsweetened almond milk (I like Malk)
Dried parsley for topping (optional)

*Makes approx 6-8 cakes

DIRECTIONS:
In a non-stick pan, melt the cream cheese and almond milk together. This step will take only a minute (be careful not to burn). Stir the melted mixture into your cold potatoes. Mix well. Form small round patties in hands. Place approx 2 to 4 potato cakes inside your air fryer at a time. Set the air fryer to 350 degrees and place the timer on for 15 minutes or adjust temp and timer to suit your fryer. Carefully remove cakes with a spatula and add your dried parsley on top. I enjoy these potato cakes with a side of organic ketchup.

HOW IN THE WORLD IS THAT VEGAN & GLUTEN-FREE?!

Cream Cheese FRUIT DIP

What a sweet and simple dip to serve with any variety of fruit! I also enjoy dipping potato chips in this.

WHAT YOU'LL NEED:
1 cup Suzanne's ricemellow crème
1/2 cup vegan cream cheese (any brand of your choosing)
1 Tbsp orange juice

*Serves 4

DIRECTIONS:
In small bowl, thoroughly mix ingredients together. Serve and Enjoy!

Mozzarella CHEESE and GARLIC Biscuits

WHAT YOU'LL NEED:
3 cups gluten-free corn bread mix (I like Bob's Redmill)
1 cup shredded vegan mozzarella (I highly recommend Violife)
1/2 tsp organic garlic powder
1 cup organic unsweetened almond milk (I like Malk)
3 Tbsp of melted vegan butter (I use Miyoko's)
2 Tbsp organic canola oil
1/2 tsp sea salt
Dried parsley for topping

*Serves 6-8

Very little effort needed to make these delicious goodies.

DIRECTIONS:
Preheat oven to 400 degrees. Line a baking sheet with parchment paper. In a medium mixing bowl, combine corn bread mix, mozzarella, and garlic powder. Add the milk, butter, oil, and sea salt and mix well. Drop large spoonfuls of batter onto baking sheet (makes approx 9 biscuits). Sprinkle parsley on top and bake for 15-18 minutes or until knife comes out clean. Remove from oven and top each biscuit with some additional butter and parsley. Enjoy these warm!

SPECTACULAR SAUSAGE SPAGHETTI SAUCE

WHAT YOU'LL NEED:
2 Tbsp organic olive oil
1 pkg Beyond Meat Beyond Sausage in Hot Italian
1 1/2 Tbsp dried minced onion
2 cups organic strained tomatoes (I recommend Bionaturae)
2 Tbsp vegan butter (I always use Miyoko's)
1/4 cup unsweetened almond milk (I love Malk)
1/2 tsp Italian seasoning
1/4 tsp garlic powder (more or less to taste)
2 Tbsp organic brown sugar (adjust sweetness to your taste)
1 tsp sea salt (more or less to taste)
3/4 tsp pepper (more or less to taste)

*Serves 4-5

This is one awesome sauce! If you love sausage, this is for you!

DIRECTIONS:
Open your Beyond Sausage package and slice down the center of each link to remove outer skin. Pour olive oil into a non-stick fry pan. Over medium heat, brown your sausage and break apart into small pieces (approx 6 minutes). Add the minced onion while browning. Once it's cooked, place the sausage into a small saucepan. Over medium-high heat, add in the rest of the ingredients and stir thoroughly bringing the sauce to a boil. Reduce and let simmer for approx 15 minutes. Start cooking your gluten-free pasta of choice while you wait. Taste the sauce and adjust the seasonings to your liking. That's all there is to it! Enjoy this incredibly hearty and delicious sauce!

ENTRÉES

HOW IN THE WORLD IS THAT VEGAN & GLUTEN-FREE?!

AMAZING AVOCADO BURGER CLUB

WHAT YOU'LL NEED:
1 Beyond Meat Beyond Burger Patty
2 slices Violife Cheddar
1 organic avocado
1 organic tomato
3 slices vegan & gluten-free bread (I like Little Northern Bakehouse)
1 Tbsp vegan mayo (I like Veganaise Soy Free)
Salt and Pepper to Taste
4 inch toothpicks to hold club together

*Serves 1

DIRECTIONS:
Slice your tomato into thin slices. Cut avocado in half and scoop out onto separate plate. With a fork, mash avocado until desired consistency and add salt and pepper to taste. Follow instructions on burger to cook for approx 6 minutes. When burger is almost finished cooking, toast your bread. Generously lather on the mayo on one side of each slice of bread. On the bottom piece of bread, place one slice of cheese followed by burger and another slice of cheese. Place non-mayo side on top of second piece of cheese. Layer your mashed avocado followed by tomato slices and add final slice of bread. Place your toothpicks around top of bread slice. I place one toothpick per side of bread. Slice sandwich on diagonal. Take out 2 toothpicks and use only one per sandwich half. Serve and Enjoy!

This burger is why I named the book "How in the World is that Vegan AND Gluten-Free?" It's absolutely amazing to have so many wonderful alternative options nowadays! You could serve this to anyone and they wouldn't know it was Plant-Based.

Pineapple Onion FAJITAS

Who says that fajitas have to be just chicken, steak, or seafood?! Feel free to add peppers or any other veggie that appeals!

WHAT YOU'LL NEED:

1 cup of organic Masa Harina flour
   (I highly recommend Bob's Redmill)
1 can of organic pineapple chunks
1 large organic sweet onion
1 cup of organic long grain rice
1 can of organic black beans (or any bean of your choosing)
1 organic lime
1/2 tsp of dried organic cilantro
Salt, pepper, and garlic to taste

* Serving Size 1-2

DIRECTIONS:

First, follow the instructions on the Masa Harina flour exactly. In my experience, one cup of flour makes 5 corn tortillas. Let the tortillas steam in a warmer and start on the rice. Make the rice according to your package. Once the rice has rested, fluff with a fork and then add 1/2 of a lime juiced and the cilantro. Mix well and season to taste then cover with lid. Chop your onions into larger sections and place in a non-stick pan. Over medium to high heat, cook the onions until translucent (approx 5 minutes). Next, add your pineapple to the onions and stir well for about 3 minutes. Finally, heat up your beans and season them to taste. I like to build the fajitas starting with the pineapple and onions on the bottom. I then add the rice and beans on top. You can add additional ingredients to make the fajitas specific to your taste. Serve and enjoy this awesome meal!

CREAMY SPINACH PENNE

This is such a delicious and filling dish. So much flavor and very simple to make!

WHAT YOU'LL NEED:
1 pkg gluten-free organic penne (I use Bionaturae)
1 pkg organic baby spinach (I use Olivia's 5 oz)
4 tsp of organic shallots (I use Christopher Ranch brand jar)
3 Tbsp organic olive oil
1/2 of Miyoko's Vegan Cultured Butter package (cut into 3 parts)
1 cup unsweetened almond milk (I use Malk)
2 Tbsp vegan cream cheese (I use Miyoko's Plainly Classic for this dish)
1 tsp organic cane sugar
Salt and pepper to taste

*Serves 4

DIRECTIONS:
Follow the cooking instructions on your pasta box and drain when finished. Place pasta back into saucepan and start on sauce. In a large non-stick fry pan on medium heat, add olive oil and shallots for only a minute and then add baby spinach. Stir spinach in pan to wilt and also add one part butter to your spinach mixture and turn heat to low. Pour in your almond milk and stir. Add your cream cheese and stir well. Once blended, add your sugar, salt, and pepper to taste. Pour sauce over your pasta and mix well making sure all penne is coated. Add additional salt and pepper to taste. Enjoy!

HOW IN THE WORLD IS THAT VEGAN & GLUTEN-FREE?!

WONDERFUL BELGIAN WAFFLES

WHAT YOU'LL NEED:

3/4 cup Sweet Rice Flour
3/4 cup Brown Rice Flour
3/4 cup Tapioca Flour
3/4 cup Garbanzo Bean Flour
2 Tbsp baking Powder
1/2 tsp sea salt
1 tsp apple cider vinegar
1 tsp vanilla extract
1 3/4 cup unsweetened almond milk (I use Malk)
1/4 cup coconut oil (melted)
1/4 cup vegan butter melted (I use Miyoko's)

* Serving Size 4 waffles

Who doesn't love a good waffle! This waffle recipe is sure to please the whole family. Add blueberries, chocolate chips, or whatever you enjoy to this batter.

DIRECTIONS:

In a large mixing bowl, combine the flours, baking powder, and sea salt. Mix thoroughly with a whisk. Next, add the apple cider vinegar, vanilla extract, almond milk (at room temp.) and whisk well. Finally, add the coconut oil and butter and whisk all together. Batter should be a medium thick consistency. Let batter rest for 5 minutes as your waffle iron heats up. With a soup ladle, pour batter in the center or your iron. Follow the timing of your own waffle maker. Serve and enjoy!

AVOCADO TOAST

This is my go to meal for breakfast, brunch, lunch, snack, or dinner. This super healthy and delicious toast is so satisfying you will crave it often!

WHAT YOU'LL NEED:
2 slices of vegan and gluten-free bread (I use Little Northern Bakehouse)
2 tsp of vegan mayo (I like Follow Your Heart Brand)
1 organic avocado
2 Tbsp organic alfalfa sprouts
1 small organic tomato sliced
Salt and pepper to taste

*Serves 1-2

DIRECTIONS:
Toast your bread and generously add the vegan mayo to it. Cut your avocado in half and spoon out onto separate plate. Add salt and pepper to taste and mix/mash the avocado to your desired consistency. Spoon mashed avocado onto your toast. Add a few sprouts and place a sliced tomato on top. Salt and pepper your tomato and serve.

WHAT YOU'LL NEED:
1 pkg Beyond Meat Beyond Sausages in Hot Italian (I use 2 links for this recipe)
1 cup organic long grain rice
1 Tbsp organic chopped garlic (I like Christopher Ranch jar)
3 Tbsp organic olive oil
1/4 cup chopped organic scallions
Garlic powder, salt, and pepper to taste

*Serves 2-3

DIRECTIONS:
Follow directions on your rice package and cook rice. Place your rice in the refrigerator for at least 2 hours. Slice your scallions. When rice is cold, put olive oil in a non-stick fry pan and follow instructions on cooking sausage. Once sausages are done, remove from heat and slice into even pieces. Remove outer casing from slices. In the same pan you cooked your sausage and on medium heat, place chopped garlic into oil for a few seconds and then add your cold rice. Stir thoroughly. Add sausages and scallions to pan and mix well. Add the garlic powder, salt, and pepper to suit your taste. Enjoy this delicious meal!

ENTRÉES

HOW IN THE WORLD IS THAT VEGAN & GLUTEN-FREE?!

HOMEMADE ORGANIC CORN TORTILLAS with "Beef"

WHAT YOU'LL NEED:
1 pkg Beyond Meat Beyond Burgers (2 Burger Patties)
Bob's Redmill Organic Golden Masa Harina Flour
Taco seasonings - Cumin, Chile Pepper, Black Pepper, Salt, Garlic Powder, Onion Powder, Dried Oregano, Red Pepper Flakes, Minced Onion (Optional), Tomato Sauce (optional)
Any fresh taco toppings you desire

*Serves 2

DIRECTIONS:

FOR THE HOMEMADE CORN TORTILLAS:
Follow the instructions on the Masa Harina EXACTLY. It says to let the dough rest for an hour and sometimes people want to skip this rest period but please don't. This time allows your dough to be perfect and not sticky when you are ready to roll it into golf ball sized pieces. Use your tortilla press with 2 sheets of parchment paper cut to the size of your press. You can also cut a gallon Ziploc bag to fit. Once you have made your tortillas, make sure you cover them in a cloth napkin or tortilla warmer to continue to steam.

FOR THE "BEEF":
In a non-stick pan, break apart the two patties of Beyond Burger and brown. Add your taco seasonings to your specific taste while the meat is cooking. Add a small amount of tomato sauce (completely optional) and continue to stir. Once finished, layer your tacos with the meat and any additional toppings. Enjoy!!

You will never buy store bought tortillas after making your own! Invest about 20 bucks in a tortilla press and it will more than pay for itself after a few "Taco Tuesdays".

HOW IN THE WORLD IS THAT VEGAN & GLUTEN-FREE?!

CHEESY GARLIC ALFREDO PASTA

This recipe is the fastest way I know how to make a terrific garlic alfredo sauce. Only 5 products used to make this absolutely yummy and satisfying dairy, gluten, and soy-free meal.

WHAT YOU'LL NEED:

Gluten-Free pasta of your choosing
2 Tbsp Miyoko's Biergarten Garlic Chive Roadhouse Cheese Spread
1 Tbsp Miyoko's Plainly Classic Vegan Cream Cheese
1/4 of one package of Miyoko's Cultured Vegan Butter
1/4 cup unsweetened almond milk - (I like the brand Malk)
Salt and pepper to taste

* Serving Size 2

DIRECTIONS:

Follow package instructions for your pasta then cook and drain. Return pasta to your saucepan and start on sauce. In a small pan, melt together on medium heat all the remaining ingredients for approx 2 minutes. Pour over pasta and mix well adding salt and pepper to taste and that's it! Perfect plant-based meal!

5-Ingredient Stovetop MAC N CHEESE

Nothing says comfort food like Mac n Cheese. This is a super fast Plant-Based meal that everyone will enjoy!

WHAT YOU'LL NEED:
1 pkg of gluten-free pasta of your choosing
1/4 cup of vegan butter (I highly recommend Miyoko's Vegan Butter)
1 cup of Violife shredded cheddar
1 cup of Violife shredded mozzarella
1 1/4 cup unsweetened almond milk (I prefer Malk)
Salt, pepper, garlic powder, etc. to taste

*Serves 4

DIRECTIONS:
Cook and drain your pasta according to its directions and set aside in the pan you cooked it in. In a small non-stick pan over medium heat, melt your butter and add both of your cheeses while stirring. Once it is blended, add the almond milk and let simmer for a few minutes. Pour over your pasta and mix well. Season the pasta to your taste. That's all there is to it! Serve and enjoy!

HOW IN THE WORLD IS THAT VEGAN & GLUTEN-FREE?!

SENSATIONAL SLOPPY JOES

WHAT YOU'LL NEED:
1 pkg Beyond Meat Beyond Burgers (2 patties)
1/2 cup organic strained tomatoes (I love Bionaturae)
1/3 cup organic ketchup
2 tsp organic light brown sugar
1 1/2 tsp apple cider vinegar
1/2 tsp salt (more or less to taste)
4 tsp dried minced onions (divided)
1/8 tsp garlic powder
1/8 tsp Italian seasoning blend
1/2 tsp pepper to taste (more or less to taste)

* Serving Size 2 (double or triple recipe to suit your family size)

DIRECTIONS:
In a small bowl, mix all ingredients for sauce (only 1 tsp of minced onion) together and season to taste. Cover with plastic wrap and place in refrigerator for a few hours for flavors to blend. In a non-stick pan over medium heat, place Beyond Burgers and mash apart. Add remaining minced onions to burger meat. Sauté for a few minutes until meat has browned (approx 5 minutes). Pour your Sloppy Joe sauce on top and mix for another 2-3 minutes and serve!

CLASSIC CHOCOLATE CHIP COOKIES

WHAT YOU'LL NEED:
1 1/4 cup gluten-free flour blend (I use Bob's Redmill 1 to 1 baking)
3/4 tsp baking soda
3/4 tsp baking powder
1/2 tsp salt
1/3 cup unsweetened almond milk (I use Malk)
1/4 cup organic cane sugar
1/4 cup organic light brown sugar
1/4 cup organic maple syrup
1 1/2 tsp vanilla extract
1/4 cup vegan butter melted (I use Miyoko's)
1/4 cup coconut oil melted
3/4 cup vegan semi sweet chocolate chips (I use Enjoy life mini)

*Makes approx 15 large cookies

Everyone needs a delicious chocolate chip cookie recipe! Watch them disappear as soon as you put them out.

DIRECTIONS:
Preheat your oven to 350 degrees. In a mixing bowl, add the flour, baking soda, baking powder, and salt. Stir the dry ingredients well. Add the almond milk, sugars, maple syrup, vanilla extract, butter, and coconut oil. Stir well to combine and then add the chocolate chips. With your hands, take a chunk of cookie dough and form the cookie shape in your palm by pressing the cookie dough firmly until its compact. This step is important to prevent the cookie from crumbling once it's baked. Please note your hands will be very oily but your final product will not be. Place formed cookies on a non-stick baking sheet and bake for 20 minutes. Let the cookies cool completely before diving in!

DESSERTS

HOW IN THE WORLD IS THAT VEGAN & GLUTEN-FREE?!

BLISSFUL BANANA BREAD

WHAT YOU'LL NEED:

DRY:
1 1/2 cup gluten-free flour blend (I use Bob's Redmill 1 to 1 baking flour)
1 cup organic brown sugar
1 tsp baking soda
1 tsp baking powder
1/2 tsp sea salt

WET:
2 ripe organic bananas
1 Tbsp apple cider vinegar
1 tsp vanilla extract
1/3 cup organic canola oil
1 Tbsp organic coconut oil (solid)
1/2 cup very cold water
1 Tbsp mini semi sweet vegan chocolate chips (optional and I like Enjoy life brand)

* Serving Size 6-8

This is fabulous banana bread! Super moist and comes out perfect every single time! It tastes truly amazing with a few vegan chocolate chips thrown in.

DIRECTIONS:

Preheat oven to 350 degrees. Spray or grease glass or non-stick bread pan. In a medium bowl, mix your dry ingredients together and set aside. In another bowl, place peeled bananas and all other ingredients except the chocolate chips. With a masher tool, mash everything until smooth. Dump your wet ingredients into the already mixed dry ingredients. Mix thoroughly and add chocolate chips or anything else of your choosing to the batter. Pour into your bread ban and bake for 60 minutes. Make sure a toothpick comes out clean. Remove and let cool before slicing. Serve and enjoy!

CINNAMON SUGAR CORN TORTILLAS
with Chocolate Chip Cream Cheese Dip

WHAT YOU'LL NEED:

FOR THE CORN TORTILLA CHIPS:
1 cup organic Masa Harina flour (I use Bob's Redmill)
1 cup hot water
Pinch of salt
1/4 cup vegan butter (I highly recommend Miyoko's)
2 Tbsp organic cane sugar
2 Tbsp organic ground cinnamon

FOR THE CHOCOLATE CHIP CREAM CHEESE DIP:
2 oz vegan cream cheese (I use Violife for this recipe)
1/4 cup organic powdered sugar
Leftover butter from tortilla chips
2 Tbsp vegan mini chocolate chips (I love enjoy life brand)

*Serves 3-4

My family is obsessed with these! They are also a perfect treat for entertaining.

DIRECTIONS:

Follow all the instructions on the package of the Masa Harina flour to make your homemade tortillas. You will use the hot water and salt in the making of the dough. Plan ahead as the dough needs to rest for 1 hour before making your tortillas. Preheat your oven to 350 degrees. Once you have made your tortillas, cut each one in half using a pizza cutter. Then cut the halves into thirds. Melt the butter into a bowl and on a separate plate mix the cinnamon and sugar together. Take each piece of tortilla and dip into the butter and then into the cinnamon sugar mix. Place them onto a baking sheet lined with parchment paper. Bake for 8-10 minutes. Remove from the oven and with a spatula remove the pieces and place onto a plate to let cool for 15 minutes. For your dip, mix the leftover butter with the cream cheese and powdered sugar. Once combined, add your chocolate chips and refrigerate for approx 10 minutes. Serve and enjoy!

CHOCOLATE CUPCAKES
with Buttercream Icing

WHAT YOU'LL NEED:
1 1/2 cups gluten-free flour (I use Bobs Redmill 1 to 1 Baking flour)
1 cup organic cane sugar
2 large heaping tablespoons of raw cacao powder (I use Navitas)
1 teaspoon baking soda
1/2 teaspoon salt
1/3 cup organic canola oil
1 teaspoon vanilla
1 teaspoon white vinegar
1 cup cold water
1/4 cup of dairy free mini chocolate chips (I use Enjoy Life)

*Serving Size 12 cupcakes

DIRECTIONS:
Preheat oven to 350 degrees. Line cupcake pan with papers or spray with nonstick baking spray. In medium bowl, stir all dry ingredients for approx 1 min. The raw cacao sometimes gets lumps so this step will help blend it in. Add the canola oil, vanilla, vinegar, and water to your dry ingredients and stir by hand making sure not to over mix. Stir in your chocolate chips. The batter will be slightly thick. Spoon the batter into your cupcake pan and bake for 18- 20 minutes. Test your cupcakes with a knife to make sure it comes out clean. Allow to cool and then frost them. See Buttercream Frosting recipe on the next page. If you didn't want icing, you can dust tops with organic powdered sugar.

DESSERTS

HOW IN THE WORLD IS THAT VEGAN & GLUTEN-FREE?!

EASY BUTTERCREAM ICING

Super simple and just delicious! This is the perfect topping for my Chocolate Cupcakes.

WHAT YOU'LL NEED:
2 cups organic powdered sugar
4 Tbsp Miyoko's Cultured Vegan Butter
2 Tbsp unsweetened almond milk (I prefer Malk)
A splash of organic vanilla extract
A pinch of sea salt

*Serving size for 12 cupcakes

DIRECTIONS:
In small mixing bowl, blend together all ingredients on low speed gradually increasing to high speed for approx 2 minutes or until all lumps have disappeared. Icing is ready when consistency is smooth and velvety.

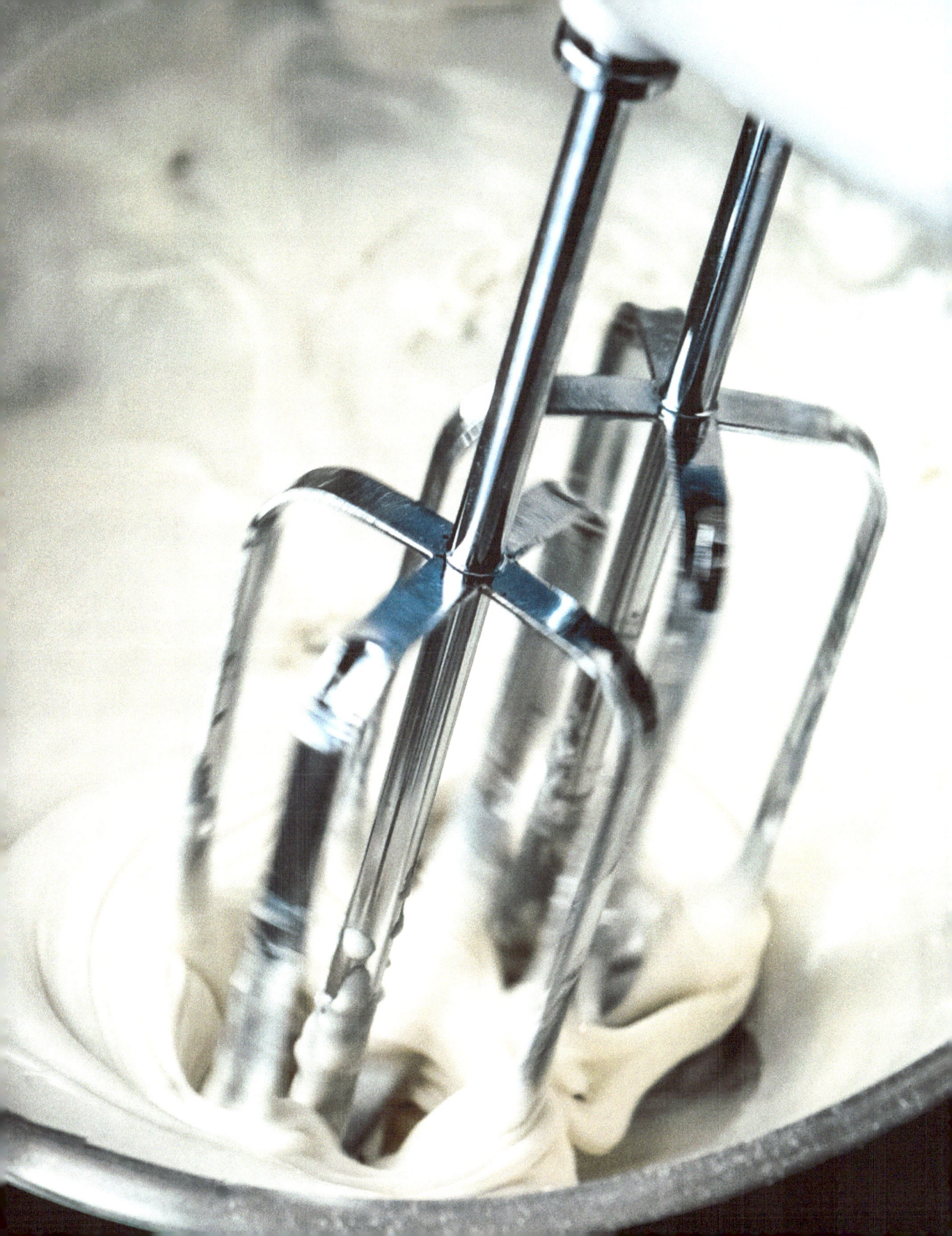

CARROT CAKE
with Cream Cheese Glaze

WHAT YOU'LL NEED:

1 cup finely shredded organic carrots
1/2 cup organic raisons
1/2 cup organic brown sugar
1/2 cup organic cane sugar
1 Tbsp apple cider vinegar
3 Tbsp very cold water
1/3 cup organic canola oil
1 Tbsp coconut oil (solid)
1/2 cup organic unsweetened applesauce

2 tsp vanilla extract
1 1/4 cup gluten-free flour blend
   (I like Bob's Redmill 1 to 1 Baking flour)
1 tsp baking soda
1/2 tsp sea salt
1/4 tsp nutmeg
2 tsp cinnamon
1 tsp orange zest (optional but highly recommend)

*Serving Size 6

For Cream Cheese Glaze:
3 oz vegan cream cheese (I love Violife), 2 cups organic powdered sugar, 2 Tbsp vegan butter, 2 Tbsp unsweetened almond milk, pinch of sea salt

DIRECTIONS:

Preheat oven to 350 degrees. Grease bottom of 9 inch pie dish. In small bowl, place your carrots and raisons and mix in a few tablespoons of flour to coat them then set aside. In another small bowl, place your dry ingredients and stir. In medium bowl, combine sugars, oils, applesauce, vanilla extract, apple cider vinegar, water and whisk thoroughly. Add the dry ingredients to your medium bowl and stir. Next, add the carrots and raisons and orange zest and mix batter well. Pour batter into pie dish and bake for 35 minutes or until toothpick comes out clean. When fully cooked, turn off oven and leave cake in oven to rest for an additional 30 minutes. Let cool and start on your cream cheese glaze. Combine all ingredients for glaze and with a hand mixer beat until smooth and velvety. Spread the delicious cream cheese glaze on top of carrot cake. I like to cut cake in half then stack the slices as pictured. Enjoy!

HOW IN THE WORLD IS THAT VEGAN & GLUTEN-FREE?!

Chocolate Covered FROZEN BANANA BITES with Sea Salt

WHAT YOU'LL NEED:
1 cup vegan chocolate chips (I only use Enjoy Life Semi Sweet)
1 Tbsp organic coconut oil
2 organic bananas
1/2 tsp sea salt
Straws

* Serving Size 3

DIRECTIONS:
Line a freezer safe plate with parchment paper. Peel bananas and cut into 1/2 inch slices. Place banana slices on parchment paper. Cut your straws into 3 parts. Insert straw piece into center of banana slice. Be careful the straw doesn't poke all the way through. Freeze bananas for at least 2 hours. After bananas are frozen, fill a saucepan half way with water and turn on medium-low heat. Place a stainless steel mixing bowl on top of saucepan to allow the water to heat and melt your chocolate. Place the chocolate chips and coconut oil in bowl and mix thoroughly. Make sure the chocolate doesn't burn. Once there are no lumps in chocolate, turn burner off. Take the individual frozen banana bites and dip into chocolate then return to parchment paper. Immediately sprinkle a little sea salt on each piece before the chocolate fully hardens. Once all pieces are dipped, return to freezer for approx ten minutes. Take out banana bites and watch your family devour them!

HOW IN THE WORLD IS THAT VEGAN & GLUTEN-FREE?!

FUDGE BROWNIES

WHAT YOU'LL NEED:
1/2 cup gluten-free flour blend (I like Bob's Redmill 1 to 1 baking flour)
1/4 cup cacao powder (I like Navitas)
1 tsp baking soda
1 tsp baking powder
1/2 tsp salt
1 cup organic cane sugar
1 cup organic apple sauce
1 tsp vanilla extract
1 tsp apple cider vinegar
3 Tbsp organic coconut oil (solid)
3 Tbsp vegan mini semi sweet chocolate chips (I love Enjoy Life brand)

* Serving Size 6

DIRECTIONS:
Preheat oven to 350 degrees. Spray bottom of a glass dish (9x7 or 8x8). In a small bowl, sift the flour and cacao powder and then add the baking soda, baking powder, and salt. Mix well and set aside. In a medium bowl, add the sugar, apple sauce, apple cider vinegar, and coconut oil. With a hand mixer beat mixture for approx 2 minutes. Next, add the dry ingredients and stir by hand. Mix in the chocolate chips to the batter and pour into your baking dish. Bake for 30 minutes and shut off oven leaving brownies to rest for another 20 minutes. Serve and enjoy!!

Vanilla and Chocolate MILKSHAKES

I always like to share the good news when I find a great product. Almond DREAM is that product when it comes to a delicious non-dairy ice cream.

WHAT YOU'LL NEED:

FOR THE VANILLA MILKSHAKE:
1 pint of Almond DREAM Vanilla
3/4 cup unsweetened almond milk
1/4 tsp organic vanilla extract

*Serving Size 1-2

FOR THE CHOCOLATE MILKSHAKE:
1 pint of Almond DREAM Chocolate
3/4 cup unsweetened almond milk
1/4 tsp organic vanilla extract
A pinch of sea salt

*Serving Size 1-2

DIRECTIONS:

Blend ingredients together for approximately 1 minute. Serve and enjoy this wonderful indulgence!

HOW IN THE WORLD IS THAT VEGAN & GLUTEN-FREE?!

Warm CINNAMON BANANA Delight

This is just so yummy and so EASY to make. It is a fantastic way to use up those ripe bananas in your home.

WHAT YOU'LL NEED:

1 organic banana (preferably ripe)
2 Tbsp Miyoko's Vegan Cultured Butter
3 tsp organic cane sugar (add more or less to suit taste)
1 tsp of ground cinnamon
1 small splash of vanilla extract
1 small pinch of sea salt

*Serving Size 1

DIRECTIONS:

Peel banana and remove all excess banana "strings". Slice your banana into even pieces. In a small pan, melt the butter and sugar together on medium-low heat for about 1 minute. Add your banana to the pan. I like to take a butter knife and stir the banana while chopping it into smaller pieces as it cooks. Add your cinnamon, vanilla extract, and sea salt. Continue to mix until it starts to bubble. Remove from heat and let it rest for 5 minutes. Serve and enjoy!

SCRUMPTIOUS BREAD PUDDING

WHAT YOU'LL NEED:
6 slices of plant-based bread (I use Little Northern Bakehouse Cinnamon Raisin)
2 cups non-dairy milk
1/2 cup organic light brown sugar
1/2 cup organic cane sugar
1 tsp ground cinnamon
1/4 tsp nutmeg
1 tsp vanilla extract
1/3 cup coconut oil melted
1/3 cup vegan cream cheese (I only use Violife for this dish)
1/3 cup vegan butter melted (I only use Miyoko's)

*Serving Size 6

DIRECTIONS:
Preheat oven to 350 degrees. Grease a 9x7 glass dish (8x8 or 9x9 will also work) with coconut oil. In a large bowl, rip up your bread slices into small pieces. In another bowl, place all of the remaining ingredients. With a hand blender mix well until everything is smooth. Pour blended mixture over the bread pieces. Press bread down with a fork to soak. Place the bread pudding mixture into your dish. Bake for 45 minutes. Serve warm or refrigerate for an awesome cold dessert.

AMAZING BLUEBERRY CHEESECAKE SMOOTHIE

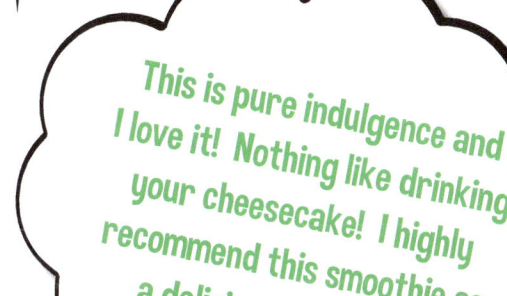

This is pure indulgence and I love it! Nothing like drinking your cheesecake! I highly recommend this smoothie as a delicious breakfast.

WHAT YOU'LL NEED:
1 cup organic frozen blueberries
1 cup non-dairy plant milk
2 Tbsp vegan cream cheese (I highly recommend Violife)
2 Tbsp organic cane sugar
1/4 tsp organic vanilla extract

*Serving Size 2

DIRECTIONS:
Place all ingredients into your blender and blend for approx. 1 minute. Enjoy!

HOW IN THE WORLD IS THAT VEGAN & GLUTEN-FREE?!

CHOCOLATE COVERED BANANA SMOOTHIE

How in the world can this drink be healthy?! The chocolate and banana combo equals perfection!

WHAT YOU'LL NEED:
1 1/2 organic bananas (fresh or frozen)
1 heaping tsp of raw cacao powder
1 1/2 cup unsweetened almond milk
4 tsp organic cane sugar (more or less to taste)
5 Ice Cubes (optional if using fresh bananas)
Pinch of sea salt

*Serving Size 2

DIRECTIONS:
In a blender, blend all ingredients together for approx 45 seconds. Add additional almond milk if you want a thinner consistency. Serve and Enjoy!

HOT MULLED APPLE CIDER

WHAT YOU'LL NEED:
1/2 Gallon bottle of organic unfiltered apple juice
1 whole navel orange sliced thin
1/2 cup organic brown sugar
2 Tbsp organic cane sugar (optional for additional sweetness)
3 Cinnamon Sticks
7 All spice berries
10 Whole cloves
1 Pinch of Sea Salt

*Serving Size 8

Perfect for Christmas morning!

DIRECTIONS:
Place everything in a large saucepan and simmer on medium heat for 20-30 minutes. You can simmer longer on low heat to make your house smell amazing! Include a slice of orange and a cinnamon stick in your mug for a beautiful presentation. Enjoy!

HOW IN THE WORLD IS THAT VEGAN & GLUTEN-FREE?!

ORGANIC ORANGE and PINEAPPLE SMOOTHIE

What a perfect smoothie to start your morning!

WHAT YOU'LL NEED:
1 1/2 cups organic orange juice (I only use Uncle Matt's brand)
1 cup organic frozen pineapple chunks
1 Tbsp organic cane sugar
1 organic navel orange to garnish (optional)

*Serving Size 2

DIRECTIONS:
In your blender, add all ingredients and blend until smooth. Add more orange juice if you desire a thinner consistency. Enjoy the citrus goodness!

HOW IN THE WORLD IS THAT VEGAN & GLUTEN-FREE?!

PEACHES and CREAM SMOOTHIE

WHAT YOU'LL NEED:

1 1/2 cups organic frozen sliced peaches
   (approx 10 ounces)
1 1/2 cups unsweetened almond milk
   (I always use Malk)
2 Tbsp organic cane sugar (to taste)

*Serving size 2-3

I love this smoothie as a simple and yummy breakfast.

DIRECTIONS:

Place all ingredients into a blender (I use a Vitamix). Blend for approx 90 seconds. Add additional ice if you would like a thicker smoothie. Serve and enjoy!

PERFECT CHOCOLATE MILK

No need for dairy with this delightful chocolate milk. It's so tasty and chocolaty. A favorite treat when I'm craving something sweet.

WHAT YOU'LL NEED:
2 cups unsweetened almond milk (I highly recommend Malk)
1 Tbsp raw cacao powder (I use Navitas)
1 Tbsp organic cane sugar

*Serving Size 1

DIRECTIONS:
Stir all ingredients for approx 3 minutes. The raw cacao powder takes a little longer to dissolve. Serve and enjoy!

HOW IN THE WORLD IS THAT VEGAN & GLUTEN-FREE?!

BANANA ALMOND BUTTER SMOOTHIE

This is a delicious smoothie that will keep you going until lunchtime!

WHAT YOU'LL NEED:
1 1/2 peeled organic bananas
2 Tbsp organic almond butter (I love Once Again brand)
1 1/2 cups unsweetened almond milk (I only use Malk)
4 tsp organic cane sugar (more or less can be used for your desired sweetness)

*Serving Size 1-2

DIRECTIONS:
Blend all ingredients for about 1 minute. Serve and Enjoy! I love to drink this smoothie out of a wide mouthed mason jar as pictured

REFRESHING ORGANIC LIMEADE

What a perfect drink on a hot day! Limeade is just so fresh and delicious!

WHAT YOU'LL NEED:
2 organic limes
2 cups of filtered water
2 Tbsp organic cane sugar (more or less if you like it sweet or tart)
Pinch of sea salt

*Serving Size 2

DIRECTIONS:
In a tall glass, juice your limes with a hand held juicer. Add the water, sugar, and sea salt and stir well. Refrigerate for 30 minutes or add ice to enjoy right away!

HOW IN THE WORLD IS THAT VEGAN & GLUTEN-FREE?!

ORGANIC BLUEBERRY LEMONADE

Move over strawberries because blueberries taste amazing in this refreshing lemonade!

WHAT YOU'LL NEED:

1 organic lemon
2 cups very cold filtered water
2 Tbsp organic cane sugar (more or less to taste)
1 cup organic frozen blueberries

*Serving Size 2-3

DIRECTIONS:

In a large glass, juice your lemon and add your water and sugar. Stir well until all sugar is dissolved. Add the lemonade to your blender along with the frozen blueberries. Blend on high for about a minute. Using a fine mesh strainer placed over a bowl; pour out your blueberry lemonade a little at a time. You may have to rinse the blueberry particles every so often. Ladle your drink into glasses and enjoy!

ABOUT THE AUTHOR

EILEEN BATES is an opera singer, voice and piano teacher, and photographer living in South Jersey. Eileen had dealt with a genetic hormonal disorder her entire life until she went vegan and gluten-free in 2017. After only two months on the plant-based diet, she was shocked to see all of her symptoms had disappeared like magic! She knew she would remain committed to this lifestyle and went on a mission to find vegan and gluten-free versions of the foods she had previously loved and enjoyed. Eileen found herself experimenting in the kitchen for hours developing recipes that reminded her of traditional comfort foods. She says her recipes are like a "survival guide" for those seeking delicious and satisfying foods as they transition to a plant-based and gluten-free lifestyle.

www.ingramcontent.com/pod-product-compliance
Lightning Source LLC
Chambersburg PA
CBHW050748110526
44591CB00002B/10